The Spectacular

Spider
Book

D1402469

The Spectacular

Spider Book

By Valerie Davies

Illustrated by

Simon Mendez

School Specialty® Publishing

© 2006 Andromeda Children's Books
An imprint of Pinwheel Ltd
Winchester House
259-269 Old Marylebone Road, London NW1 5XJ UK

Author: Valerie Davies
Illustrator: Simon Mendez
Design: Nicola Sokell
Editor: Emily Hawkins
American Editor: Sue Diehm
Editorial Manager: Ruth Hooper
Production Director: Clive Sparling
Publishing / Creative Director: Linda Cole

School Specialty
Publishing

This edition published in 2006 by
School Specialty Publishing,
a member of the School Specialty Family.

Library of Congress
Cataloging-in-Publication Data
is on file with the publisher.

Send all inquiries to:
School Specialty Publishing
8720 Orion Place
Columbus, OH 43240-2111

ISBN 0-7696-4429-5

1 2 3 4 5 6 7 8 9 10 PIN 10 09 08 07 06

Printed in China.

Contents

What Is a Spider?

Spiders belong to a group of animals called *arachnids*. They are *invertebrates*, which means that they do not have a backbone. They are found in many places—anywhere they can find insects to eat.

Arachnid or Insect?

This is how they are different.

Arachnid

An arachnid has eight legs and spinnerets to spin silk for its web.

Insect

An insect has six legs, wings, and antennae. It also has ears, a nose, and a tongue.

A Spider's Body

A spider's body is covered by a hard, stretchy skin called an *exoskeleton*. As the spider grows, it *molts*. It sheds its skin for a larger skin underneath.

Head and Chest

The head and chest make up the front part of the spider's body.

Body

The back part of the spider is called the *abdomen*.

Spinnerets

Spinnerets on the back of the abdomen spin silk for the spider's web.

6

Cobalt Blue Spider

A spider has two feelers.

Most spiders have eight eyes.

Spiders have jaws to bite and crush prey.

Pores on the feet help the spider sense things.

Sharp claws at the end of each leg help the spider grip surfaces.

A spider has eight hollow legs. Each leg has seven sections.

7

Spinning a Web

Some spiders build webs to help them catch food. Using a claw on its hind leg, a spider pulls silk out of its spinnerets. The liquid silk hardens into a strong, stretchy thread.

Step 1:
First, the spider casts out a thread to cross a gap. This is called the *bridge line*.

Step 2:
The spider joins a sagging line from one end of the bridge line to the other.

Step 3:
The spider drops down a thread halfway along this line, making a *Y* shape. The center of the *Y* will be the middle of the web.

Step 4:
Next, the spider spins a frame of threads, called *radials*. They look like the spokes of a bicycle wheel.

Step 6:
Finally, starting from the outside and working toward the center, the spider spins sticky circles. It eats the dry ones as it goes. A space is left in the middle where the spider can wait until an insect flies into its trap.

Step 5:
Then, starting from the center, the spider works outward. It spins circles of dry silk to hold the radials in place.

9

Web-Building Spiders

It takes about an hour to spin a web. Many spiders build a new one each night. When a spider feels movement in its web, it quickly heads toward its prey.

The yellow garden orb weaver spins a round web. It feels movement on its web with its feet.

The funnel weaver's web has a funnel-shaped hole where the spider hides, waiting to jump on its prey.

Funnel Weaver

Yellow Garden Orb Weaver

The St. Andrew's cross spider gets its name because it holds its legs in four pairs, making an *X* shape.

St. Andrew's Cross

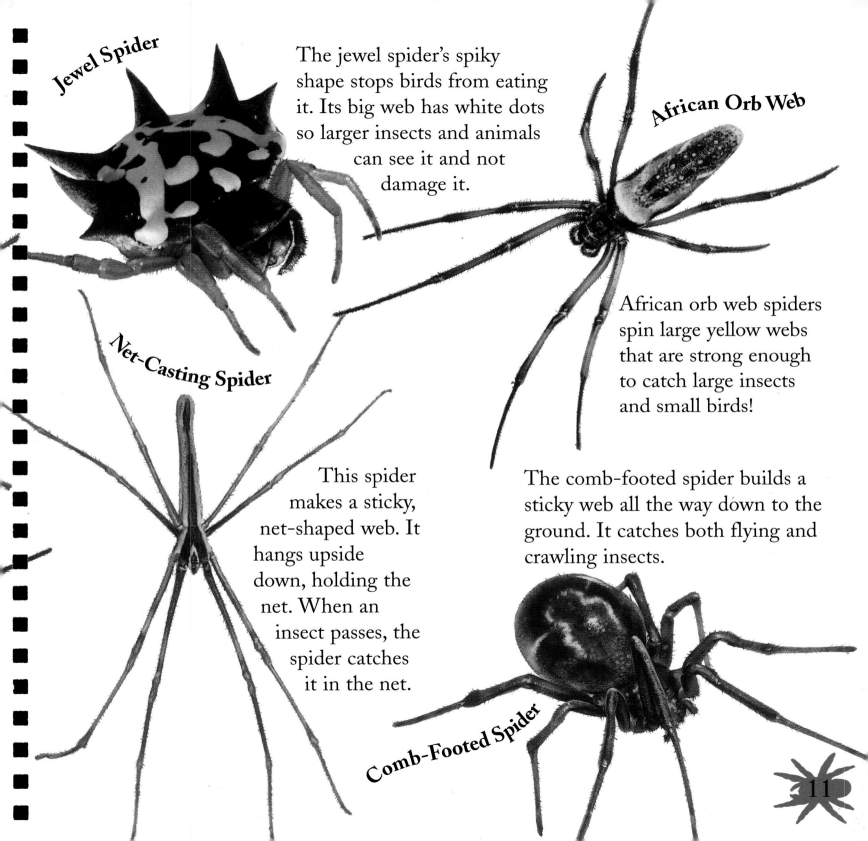

Jewel Spider

The jewel spider's spiky shape stops birds from eating it. Its big web has white dots so larger insects and animals can see it and not damage it.

African Orb Web

African orb web spiders spin large yellow webs that are strong enough to catch large insects and small birds!

Net-Casting Spider

This spider makes a sticky, net-shaped web. It hangs upside down, holding the net. When an insect passes, the spider catches it in the net.

The comb-footed spider builds a sticky web all the way down to the ground. It catches both flying and crawling insects.

Comb-Footed Spider

11

Hunters, Stalkers, and

Half of all spiders do not spin webs to catch their food. Instead, they catch prey by stalking and jumping.

The red trapdoor spider digs a hole and closes it with a trapdoor made of silk and mud. When an insect comes near, the spider rushes out and grabs it in its jaws.

Portia

A Portia spider shakes the webs of other spiders. This makes the spiders come out of their hiding places. Then, the Portia spider pounces on them.

Red Trapdoor

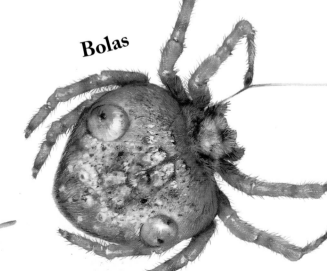

Bolas

Jumpers

Pantropical Jumping Spider

Spitting Spider

The pantropical jumping spider stalks its prey, crouches, and then pounces. It often attacks insects much larger than itself.

When the spitting spider spots an insect, it squirts two lines of poisonous gum from its fangs to pin down its prey.

Although its legs are short, the two-striped jumping spider can jump up to 40 times the length of its body!

The bolas spider catches moths by swinging a thread of silk with a sticky droplet on the end, like a fishing line and hook.

Two-Striped Jumping Spider

13

Mexican Fireleg

Giant Spiders

Tarantulas are the largest, hairiest spiders. Although they look scary, most are shy and avoid danger. Some tarantulas eat lizards, mice, and even small birds.

The Mexican fireleg stays deep in its hole during the day. It hunts at night.

Cobalt blue tarantulas are fast and aggressive. They are about 6 inches across.

Cobalt Blue

When frightened, the Usambara orange spider rears up, hisses, and drips poison from its fangs.

Usambara Orange

14

Brazilian Pink

Goliath

A Brazilian pink tarantula can flick its hairs into its enemy's face. These hairs cause the skin to itch.

Venezuelan Suntiger

Venezuelan suntiger tarantulas live in trees. They use their stiff hairs to detect insects.

The goliath is the largest spider in the world. Its leg span is nearly a foot across. It eats frogs, mice, birds, and even snakes.

15

Deadly Spiders

A spider has *venom*, or poison, in its fangs. It uses its poisonous bite to kill its prey and defend itself. About 30 species of spider are dangerous to human beings.

The violin spider looks harmless, but it often crawls into people's beds and gives them a poisonous bite.

Violin Spider

Red-Back

Only the female black widow is dangerous. Her venom is 15 times more powerful than a rattlesnake's.

The Australian red-back spider usually avoids people. Sometimes, it comes into contact with them, because it hides in buildings.

Black Widow

Brown Recluse

The sand spider hides under the sand. It can sense movement 60 feet away. When its prey gets close, it leaps out and gives a poisonous bite.

A bite from a brown recluse spider takes 6 – 8 weeks to heal. Some people have died from its bite.

Sand Spider

Brazilian Wandering Spider

One of the deadliest spiders is the Sydney funnel web spider. It lives underground, but often finds its way into people's homes.

The Brazilian wandering spider has the most deadly venom. It has enough venom to kill 220 mice or a human being!

Funnel Web

17

Mothers

Female spiders use their silk to make egg sacs. They guard the egg sacs in their webs, or carry them in their jaws or under their bodies. Baby spiders, called *spiderlings*, will hatch from the eggs.

Black Widow

A black widow spider hides her egg sac with grass and leaves. She guards it until the spiderlings hatch after 20 – 30 days.

Wolf Spider

Spiderlings of the female wolf spider cling to special hairs on her back for about 10 days after they hatch.

The nursery web spider carries her egg sac beneath the front half of her body. She uses her fangs and feelers to keep it in place.

Nursery Web

18

...and Babies

Most spiderlings break out of their eggs with a special tooth, called an *egg tooth*.

At first, they cannot feed or spin silk. About a week after they have hatched, they molt and separate from each other.

Once the spiderlings can feed and spin silk, they set off to find a home of their own. They fly off on silken threads that catch the breeze. This is called *ballooning*.

Spiderlings

19

Water Spiders

Some spiders live close to water, where they hunt, but they always eat their prey on dry land.

The water spider spins a web among water plants. It fills the web with air, so it becomes a bell-shaped bubble.

Raft Spider

Water Spider

The fishing spider sits on a floating leaf and keeps its front legs on the surface to feel movements made by small fish and insects.

Beach Wolf Spider

Raft spiders can walk on the water's surface. They use their legs to push themselves along.

Fishing Spider

The beach wolf spider lives on the seashore. It eats insects it finds in seaweed.

20

Close to Home

Many kinds of spiders live peacefully in our gardens and homes. Most are useful because they eat insect pests that can carry disease.

Cross Spider

Cross spider webs usually appear in the fall. This spider's name comes from the cross pattern on its back.

Crab Spider

Zebra Spider

The zebra spider is usually seen around houses, often on walls and window frames. It does not make a web, but stalks its prey.

Huntsman

Crab spiders live near leaves and flowers. They change color when they move from one flower to another.

Webs spun in high corners are usually the only signs of the tiny, harmless huntsman spider.

21

Fascinating Facts

Spiders have been on earth for more than 300 million years. The earliest human beings lived only 6 million years ago.

Orb weaver spiders wrap their prey in sheets like mummies so that they cannot escape.

Because spiders can store food in their stomachs, they can live more than a year without eating!

Many spiders live for only one season, but female tarantulas can live for up to 20 years.

If a spider loses a leg, it can grow it back again.

The funnel web spider can hold its breath for up to 72 hours!

There are more than 35,000 different kinds of spiders. Some are as small as the head of a pin. Others are as large as a person's hand.

Some species of spiders that live in dark places have no eyes at all!

Glossary

ABDOMEN (AB-doh-men): The back section of a spider's body.

ARACHNID (a-RAK-nid): A group of animals, including spiders, that have four pairs of legs, several eyes, but no antennae.

EGG SAC (EG SAK): A silken pouch made by a spider to keep its eggs together and stop them from drying out.

EXOSKELETON (EX-o-SKE-le-ton): A hard, flexible outer skin, or shell, that protects the soft parts of an animal.

INVERTEBRATE (in-VER-te-brayt): An animal that does not have a backbone, or spine.

MOLTING (MOLT-ing): The process of shedding an outer skin, which is then replaced by a new one from underneath.

SPINNERETS (SPIN-er-ets): Short, finger-like organs at the back of the abdomen from which silk is pulled.

VENOM (VE-nem): A poisonous liquid injected by the fangs into prey, to kill or paralyze it.

Index